TRADE CAREERS
MECHANIC

by Joanne Mattern

pogo

Ideas for Parents and Teachers

Pogo Books let children practice reading informational text while introducing them to nonfiction features such as headings, labels, sidebars, maps, and diagrams, as well as a table of contents, glossary, and index.

Carefully leveled text with a strong photo match offers early fluent readers the support they need to succeed.

Before Reading

- "Walk" through the book and point out the various nonfiction features. Ask the student what purpose each feature serves.
- Look at the glossary together. Read and discuss the words.

Read the Book

- Have the child read the book independently.
- Invite him or her to list questions that arise from reading.

After Reading

- Discuss the child's questions. Talk about how he or she might find answers to those questions.
- Prompt the child to think more. Ask: Would you like to be a mechanic? What do you like about this trade career?

Pogo Books are published by Jump!
5357 Penn Avenue South
Minneapolis, MN 55419
www.jumplibrary.com

Copyright © 2025 Jump!
International copyright reserved in all countries. No part of this book may be reproduced in any form without written permission from the publisher.

Library of Congress Cataloging-in-Publication Data

Names: Mattern, Joanne, 1963- author.
Title: Mechanic / by Joanne Mattern.
Description: Minneapolis, MN: Jump!, Inc., [2025]
Series: Trade careers | Includes index.
Audience: Ages 7-10
Identifiers: LCCN 2024002015 (print)
LCCN 2024002016 (ebook)
ISBN 9798892131643 (hardcover)
ISBN 9798892131650 (paperback)
ISBN 9798892131667 (ebook)
Subjects: LCSH: Machinery—Maintenance and repair—Vocational guidance—Juvenile literature. Mechanics (Persons)—Juvenile literature.
Classification: LCC TJ157 .M389 2025 (print)
LCC TJ157 (ebook)
DDC 629.28/7023—dc23/eng/20240216
LC record available at https://lccn.loc.gov/2024002015
LC ebook record available at https://lccn.loc.gov/2024002016

Editor: Alyssa Sorenson
Designer: Anna Peterson
Content Consultants: Paul Gleisner, Lead Industrial Mechanic; Tom Bunce, Aircraft Mechanic; Jeff Copeland, Automotive Technology Instructor, Dakota County Technical College

Photo Credits: Gregory Gerber/Shutterstock, cover (gears); vipman/Shutterstock, cover (wrench); trek6500/Shutterstock, 1; Serhii Akhtemiichuk/iStock, 3; Wavebreakmedia/iStock, 4; Monkey Business Images/Shutterstock, 5; sturti/Getty, 6-7; piemags/military23/Alamy, 8-9; Andriy Popov/Alamy, 10-11tl; welcomia/iStock, 10-11tr; Wormphoto/iStock, 10-11bl; ALPA PROD/Shutterstock, 10-11br; kali9/iStock, 12, 13; Borusikk/Dreamstime, 14-15; industryview/iStock, 16-17; Volodymyr Krasyuk/Shutterstock, 17 (jack); Jamroen_Photo Background/Shutterstock, 17 (pliers); agoIndr/Shutterstock, 17 (screwdriver); Andrii Horulko/Shutterstock, 17 (flashlight); kuzina1964/iStock, 17 (ratchets and sockets); Thammasak Lek/Shutterstock, 17 (wrench); Bruce Alan Bennett/Shutterstock, 18; Spettacolare/Dreamstime, 19; Caiaimage/Paul Bradbury/iStock, 20-21; New Africa/Shutterstock, 23.

Printed in the United States of America at Corporate Graphics in North Mankato, Minnesota.

TABLE OF CONTENTS

CHAPTER 1
What Is a Mechanic? 4

CHAPTER 2
Learning the Trade 12

CHAPTER 3
Where They Work 18

ACTIVITIES & TOOLS
Try This! 22
Glossary 23
Index 24
To Learn More 24

CHAPTER 1

WHAT IS A MECHANIC?

Mechanics fix machines. They **inspect** them. They keep them running. There are many kinds of machines. That means there are many kinds of mechanics!

Auto mechanics work on cars. They fix **brakes**. They change **engine** parts. They know how to fix all parts of a vehicle.

CHAPTER 1 5

An auto mechanic plugs a scanner into a car. It connects to the car's computer. It scans for problems. The mechanic looks at the information. She can see what is not working right. Now she knows what to fix!

DID YOU KNOW?

Cars have been around for a long time. The first school for auto mechanics opened in the early 1900s.

CHAPTER 1

Aircraft mechanics work on planes. A mechanic looks at a plane's engine. He checks for any cracks or oil leaks. He weaves a borescope between the engine's parts. Why? This is a small camera. It is attached to a thin tube. Now he can see inside the engine. He makes sure there are no problems.

CHAPTER 1

elevator mechanic

heavy equipment mechanic

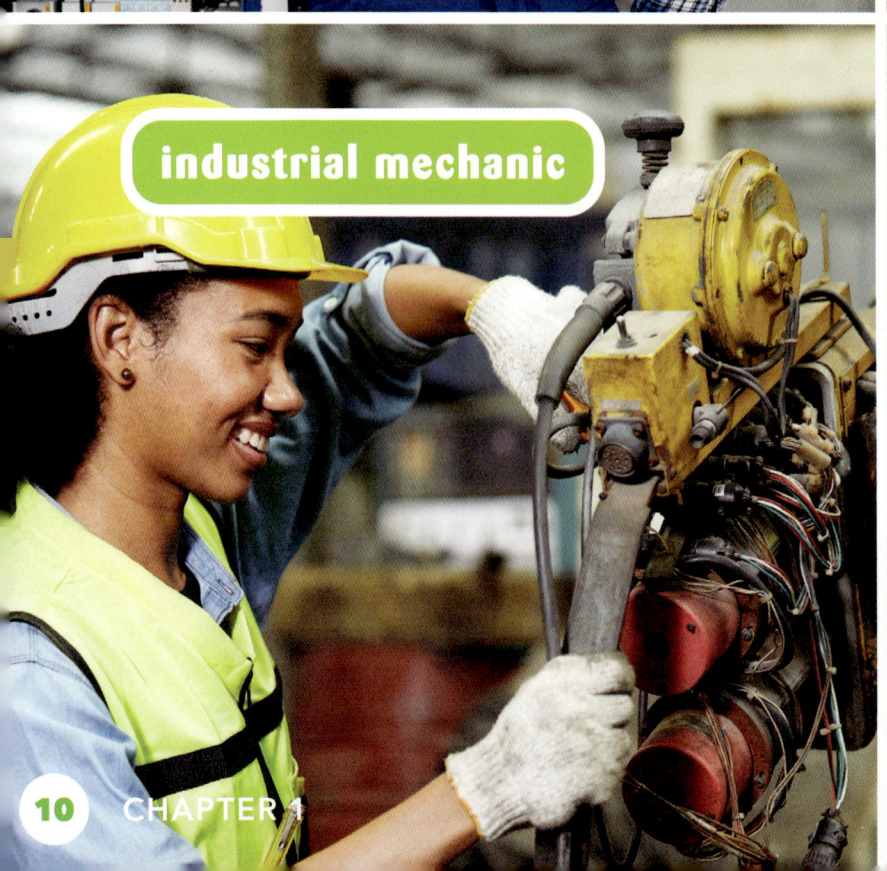
industrial mechanic

10 CHAPTER 1

Elevator mechanics put in and fix elevators. Heavy equipment mechanics work on big vehicles like bulldozers. Small engine mechanics fix smaller machines. These include snowmobiles and lawn mowers. **Industrial** mechanics make sure **factory** machines work.

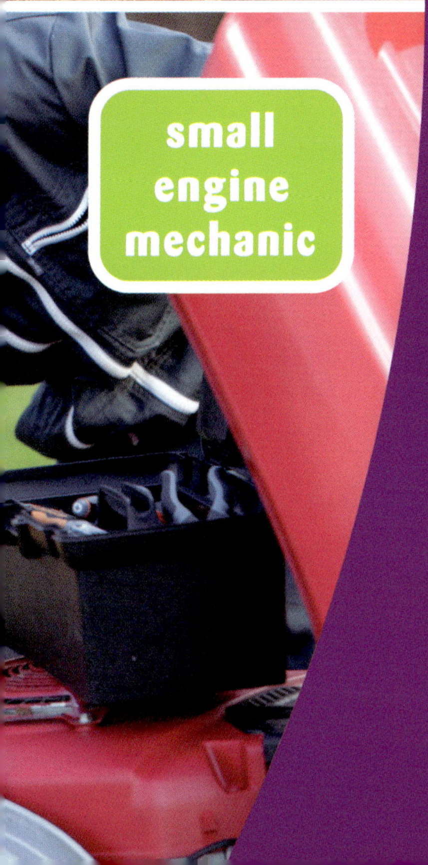

small engine mechanic

DID YOU KNOW?

Mechanics may wear coveralls. These protect their clothes. They may wear safety glasses and gloves. Glasses keep their eyes safe from oil, chemicals, and dust. Gloves protect their hands from burns and cuts.

CHAPTER 1 11

CHAPTER 2
LEARNING THE TRADE

Do you want to be a mechanic? You can take classes at a **vocational school**. You will learn important skills to work in the **trade**.

apprentice

You can also be an **apprentice**. You will work with an experienced mechanic to learn more. After your training, you can take a test. Why? If you pass, you will get a **certificate**. It shows you have the skills to be a good mechanic.

Mechanics solve problems often. Why? People don't always know why a machine isn't working. Mechanics figure out what is wrong. Then they fix it. They might try many different things. They may have to take something apart. Then they put it back together again.

> **DID YOU KNOW?**
>
> Machines have a lot of parts. Mechanics must know about all of them. They need to know how they fit and work together.

CHAPTER 2

Mechanics talk with customers. They tell them what is wrong with their machines. They explain how they will fix them.

TAKE A LOOK!

Mechanics use many tools. What are some? Take a look!

jack: lifts vehicles so mechanics can work underneath them

pliers: grabs objects and parts

screwdriver: tightens and loosens screws

flashlight: lights up dark spaces

ratchet and sockets: tightens and loosens bolts and nuts

wrench: tightens and loosens bolts and nuts

CHAPTER 2   17

CHAPTER 3

WHERE THEY WORK

Auto mechanics often work in repair shops. Some work at **dealerships**. Some work on NASCAR cars!

Heavy equipment mechanics work at repair shops. They also work outside. They go wherever machines are broken down, such as construction sites.

CHAPTER 3　19

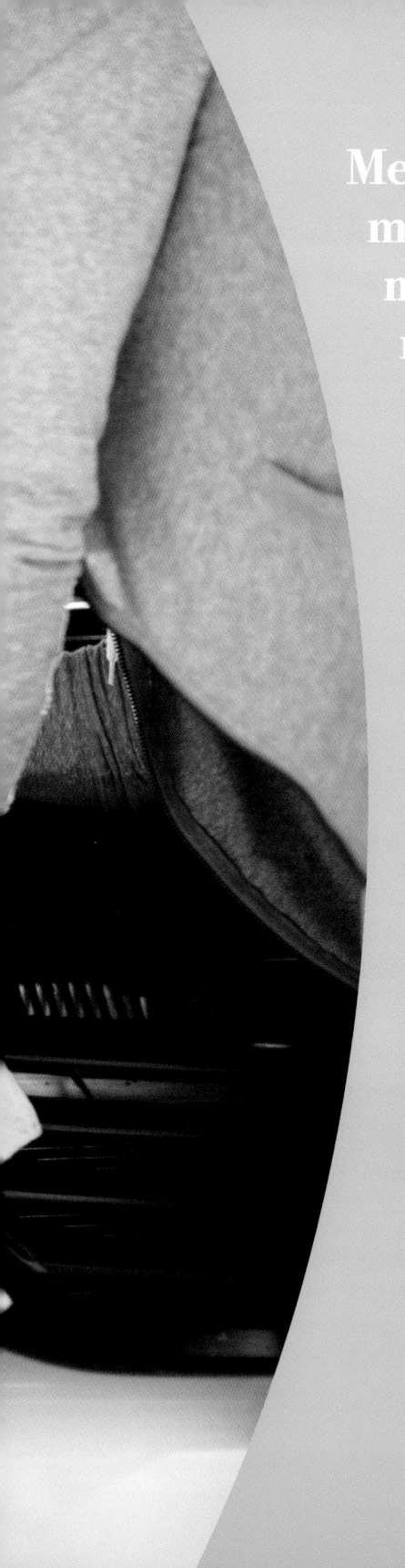

Mechanics are ready to fix any machines that break. We need mechanics. Why? They keep our machines and vehicles running!

CHAPTER 3 21

ACTIVITIES & TOOLS

TRY THIS!

BUILD A CAR

Build a car. Think like a mechanic!

What You Need:
- ruler
- plastic drinking straw
- scissors
- 2 bread ties
- 4 buttons that are the same size
- clothespin
- tape

1. Measure two 1-inch (2.54 cm) pieces of the straw. Cut the two pieces off.
2. Put a bread tie in each straw piece.
3. Loop one button onto the ends of each bread tie. The buttons are your car's wheels.
4. Clip the clothespin to the middle of one straw piece.
5. Place the second straw piece at the other end of the clothespin. Push it up against the spring.
6. Tape the back end of the clothespin. This will keep the wheels in place.
7. Push the car. Do the wheels roll? If not, what could you do to fix them?

GLOSSARY

apprentice: Someone who learns a skill by working with an expert.

brakes: Devices that slow down and stop a vehicle.

certificate: A document that shows a person has met requirements.

dealerships: Places where cars are sold.

engine: A machine that makes something move by using gasoline or another energy source.

factory: A building in which products are made in large numbers, often using machines.

industrial: Having to do with factories and making things in large quantities.

inspect: To examine something carefully.

trade: A job that requires working with the hands or with machines.

vocational school: A school that prepares students for trade careers.

ACTIVITIES & TOOLS   23

INDEX

aircraft mechanics 8
apprentice 13
auto mechanics 5, 7, 18
borescope 8
brakes 5
bulldozers 11
certificate 13
construction sites 19
coveralls 11
dealerships 18
elevator mechanics 11
engine 5, 8

heavy equipment mechanics 11, 19
industrial mechanics 11
inspect 4
NASCAR 18
planes 8
problems 7, 8, 14
repair shops 18, 19
safety glasses 11
small engine mechanics 11
test 13
tools 17
vocational school 12

TO LEARN MORE

Finding more information is as easy as 1, 2, 3.

1. Go to www.factsurfer.com
2. Enter "mechanic" into the search box.
3. Choose your book to see a list of websites.

24 ACTIVITIES & TOOLS